One Red Bicycle
Una Bicicleta R...

빨간 자전거 한 대 一辆 红色的 自行车

Explore Numbers, Colors, and Vehicles in English, Spanish, Chinese & Korean

ISBN: 978-1-949676-00-6
David Ming
Copyright © 2019 by David Yeh
Yeh! Books, a division of Yeh! Made
Everyday Concepts Vol. 1

One Red Bicycle
Una Bicicleta Roja

一辆 红色的 自行车
YīLiàng HóngSèDe ZìXíngChē
一輛 紅色的 自行車

빨간 자전거 한 대
Ppalgan Jajeongeo Han Dae

2

Two Orange Scooters
Dos Motos Anaranjadas

两辆　橙色的　电动车
LiǎngLiàng　ChéngSèDe　DiànDòngChē
兩輛　橙色的　電動車

주황색　오토바이 두 대
Juhwangsaek　Otobai　Du　Dae

Note: 二 / Èr / 二 is the number "2" and is used for arithmetic; however, when counting objects, the word 两 / Liǎng / 兩 is used instead.

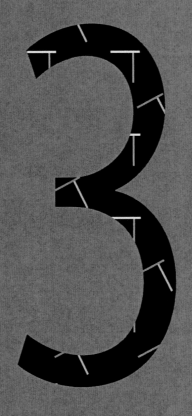

Three Black Cars
Tres Carros / Coches / Autos Negros

三辆　黑色的　汽车
SānLiàng　HēiSèDe　QìChē
三輛　黑色的　汽車

까만 자동차 세 대
Kkaman Jadongcha Se Dae

4

Four Brown Trucks
Cuatro Camiones Marrones

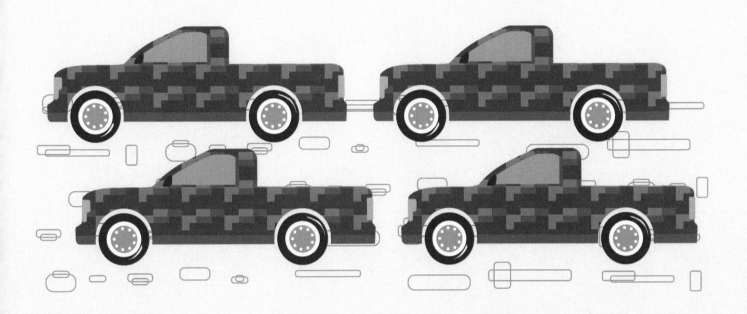

四辆 棕色的 卡车
SìLiàng ZōngSèDe KǎChē

四輛 棕色的 卡車

갈색 트럭 네 대
Galsaek Teureok Ne Dae

5

Five Green Buses
Cinco Autobuses Verdes

五辆 绿色的 公交车
WǔLiàng LǜSèDe GōngJiāoChē
五輛 綠色的 公交車

초록색 버스 다섯 대
Choroksaek Beoseu Daseot Dae

6

Six Yellow Trains
Seis Trenes Amarillos

六列 黄色的 火车
LiùLiè HuángSèDe HuǒChē
六列 黃色的 火車

노란 기차 여섯 대
Noran Gicha Yeoseot Dae

7

Seven Pink Surfboards
Siete Tablas de Surf Rosadas

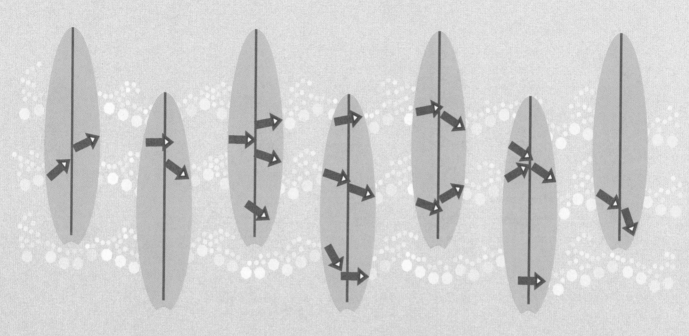

七个　粉红色的　冲浪板
QīGè　FěnHóngSèDe　ChōngLàngBǎn
七個　粉紅色的　衝浪板

분홍색　서핑　보드　일곱　개
Bunhongsaek　Seoping　Bodeu　Ilgop　Gae

Eight Blue Boats
Ocho Barcos Azules

八艘 蓝色的 船
BāSōu LánSèDe Chuán

八艘 藍色的 船

파란 배 여덟 척
Paran Bae Yeodeol Cheok

9

Nine Purple Hot Air Balloons
Nueve Globos Aerostáticos Morados

九个 紫色的 热 气球
JiǔGè ZǐSèDe Rè QìQiú
九個 紫色的 熱 氣球

보라색 열기구 아홉 대
Borasaek Yeolgigu Ahop Dae

Ten White Airplanes
Diez Aviones Blancos

十架 白色的 飞机
ShíJià BáiSèDe FēiJī

十架 白色的 飛機

하얀 비행기 열 대
Hayan Bihaenggi Yeol Dae

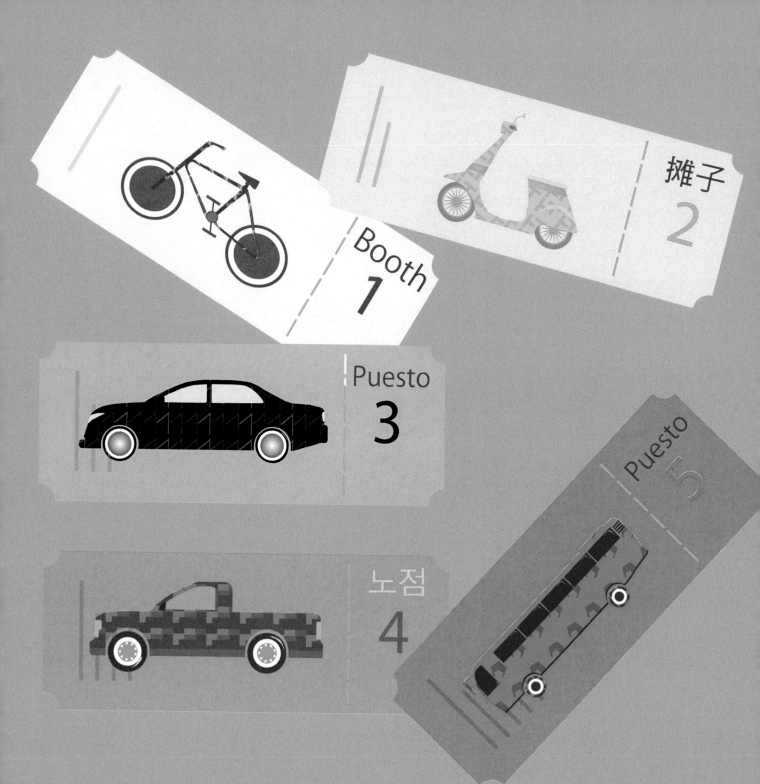

Booth
1

摊子
2

Puesto
3

노점
4

Puesto
5

攤子
6

노점
9

Booth
7

Puesto
8

노점
10

Numbers	Números	数字 / ShùZì / 數字	번호 / Beonho
		Simplified / Mandarin PīnYīn / Traditional 简体中文 / 拼音 / 繁體中文	Korean / Korean Romanization 한국어 / 로마자 표기법
1 One	Uno	一 / Yī / 一	하나* / Hana
2 Two	Dos	二* / Èr / 二*	둘* / Dul
3 Three	Tres	三 / Sān / 三	셋* / Set
4 Four	Cuatro	四 / Sì / 四	넷* / Net
5 Five	Cinco	五 / Wǔ / 五	다섯 / Daseot
6 Six	Seis	六 / Liù / 六	여섯 / Yeoseot
7 Seven	Siete	七 / Qī / 七	일곱 / Ilgop
8 Eight	Ocho	八 / Bā / 八	여덟 / Yeoldol
9 Nine	Nueve	九 / Jiǔ / 九	아홉 / Ahop
10 Ten	Diez	十 / Shí / 十	열 / Yeol

* Some numbers change form when referring to the number itself (compared to when counting).

Colors	Colores	颜色 / YánSè / 顔色	그림 물감 / Geulim Mulgam
		Simplified / Mandarin PīnYīn / Traditional 简体中文 / 拼音 / 繁體中文	Korean / Korean Romanization 한국어 / 로마자 표기법
Red	Rojo	红色 / HóngSè / 紅色	빨간색 / Ppalgansaek
Orange	Anaranjado	橙色 / ChéngSè / 橙色	주황색 / Juhwangsaek
Black	Negro	黑色 / HēiSè / 黑色	까만색 / Kkamansaek
Brown	Marrón	棕色 / ZōngSè / 棕色	갈색 / Galsaek
Green	Verde	绿色 / LǜSè / 綠色	초록색 / Choroksaek
Yellow	Amarillo	黄色 / HuángSè / 黃色	노란색 / Noransaek
Pink	Rosado	粉红色 / FěnHóngSè / 粉紅色	분홍색 / Bunhongsaek
Blue	Azul	蓝色 / LánSè / 藍色	파란색 / Paransaek
Purple	Morado	紫色 / ZǐSè / 紫色	보라색 / Borasaek
White	Blanco	白色 / BáiSè / 白色	흰색 / Huinsaek

Vehicles	Vehículos	车辆 / ChēLiàng / 車輛	운송 수단 / Unsong Sudan
		Simplified / Mandarin PīnYīn / Traditional 简体中文 / 拼音 / 繁體中文	Korean / Korean Romanization 한국어 / 로마자 표기법
Bicycle	Bicicleta	自行车 / ZìXíngChē / 自行車 脚踏车 / JiǎoTàChē / 脚踏车 单车 / DānChē / 單車	자전거 / Jajeongeo
Scooter	Moto	电动车 / DiànDòng Chē / 電動車 滑板车 / HuáBǎnChē / 滑板車 踏板车 / TàBǎnChē / 踏板車	오토바이 / Otobai
Car	Carro Coche Auto	汽车 / QìChē / 汽車	자동차 / Jadongcha
Truck	Camión	卡车 / KǎChē / 卡車	트럭 / Teureok
Bus	Autobús	公交车 / GōngJiāoChē / 公交車 公共汽车 / GōngGòngQìChē / 公共汽車	버스 / Beoseu
Train	Tren	火车 / HuǒChē / 火車	기차 / Gicha
Surfboard	Tabla de Surf	冲浪板 / ChōngLàngBǎn / 衝浪板	서핑 보드 / Seoping Bodeu
Boat	Barco	船 / Chuán / 船	배 / Bae
Hot Air Balloon	Globo Aerostático	热气球 / Rè QìQiú / 熱氣球	열기구 / Yeolgigu
Airplane	Avión	飞机 / FēiJī / 飛機	비행기 / Bihaenggi

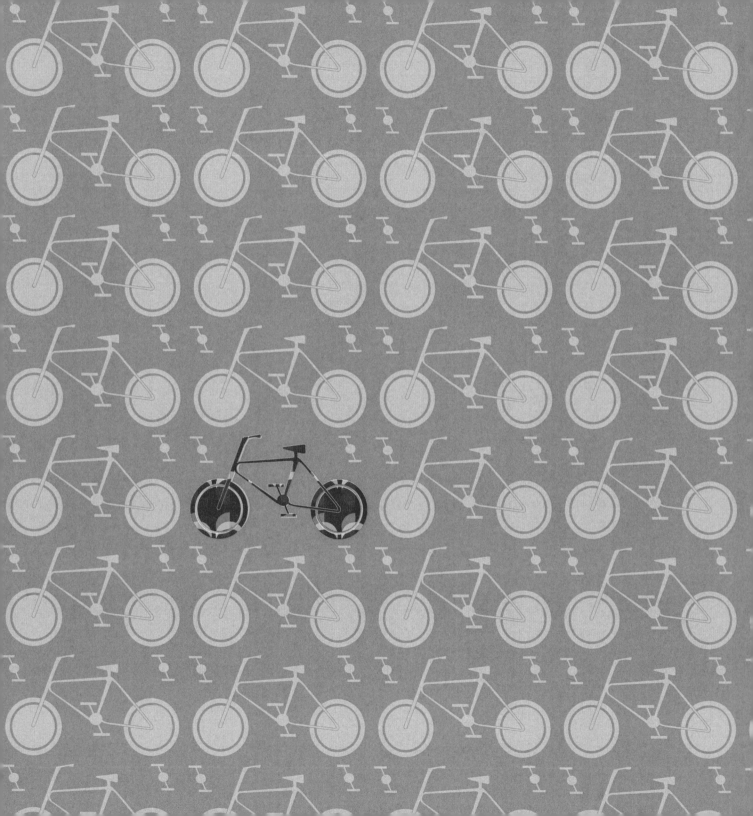

Made in the USA
Columbia, SC
15 July 2019